Copyright © 2021 Heidi Kinney
https://www.heidikinney.com
All rights reserved.

No part of this book may be reproduced, stored in a retrieval system, distributed, or transmitted in any form or by any means, including photocopying, recording, or other electronic or mechanical methods, without prior written permission of the copyright owner except for the use of brief quotations in a book review. For permission requests, contact heidi@heidikinney.com. The content of this book is not to be considered professional advice. The author assumes no responsibility on behalf of the consumer of this material. The author in no way represents or endorses any company or brand mentioned herein.
ISBN 978-1-7372557-3-4

Welcome!

Welcome to your new homeschool planner! Whether this is your first year of homeschooling or your final year, this planner is for you.

When I began homeschooling years ago, I searched for a planner that suited my needs. I wanted something that allowed for flexibility with plenty of space to write my plans. I wanted very little fluff, or forms and checklists that didn't pertain to our homeschool. As a busy homeschooling mom, I wanted a simple, effective planner.

I never found the ideal planner. For years, I used a binder filled with forms that I created myself. This worked fine, but I disliked the bulkiness of the binder. I transitioned to using an inexpensive basic teacher planner with some of my forms paper-clipped to the inside. However, there were pages in the planner that didn't pertain to our homeschool, and my forms would often fall out. To solve this problem, I created the *All I Need to Homeschool Planner*. It combines the convenience of a bound book with the tracking forms and planning pages that I have found to be the most helpful over the years. It is undated to allow for ultimate flexibility. You can use the weekly planning pages either vertically or horizontally, and I included some bonus material in the back.

I wish you much success on your homeschool journey. May this planner be the beginning of a fantastic year!

~ Heidi

Table of Contents

Goals This Year 1

First Quarter Goals 2

Second Quarter Goals 3

Third Quarter Goals 4

Fourth Quarter Goals 5

Curriculum & Supplies 6

Field Trips & Activities 8

Reading List 10

Grades 12

Reference Calendars 14

Monthly Calendars 15

Weekly Plan 21

Future Goals 125

Helpful Hints 126

Fun Diversions 127

Class Ideas for Groups 128

Homeschooling Resources 129

Author's Note 130

Goals This Year   Dates:_____

Student	Subject	Goal

First Quarter Goals   Dates: _____

Student	Subject	Goal

Second Quarter Goals   Dates:_____

Student	Subject	Goal

Third Quarter Goals   Dates:_____

Student	Subject	Goal

Fourth Quarter Goals   Dates:_____

Student	Subject	Goal

Curriculum & Supplies

Description	Have	Need	Cost	Notes

Description	Have	Need	Cost	Notes

Field Trips & Activities

Description	Cost	Notes

Description	Cost	Notes

Reading List

Student	Title	Notes

Student	Title	Notes

Grades

Student	Subject	Description	Grade

Student	Subject	Description	Grade

Reference Calendars

2024 ✦ 2025

August	September	October	November	December	January
S M T W T F S	S M T W T F S	S M T W T F S	S M T W T F S	S M T W T F S	S M T W T F S
1 2 3	1 2 3 4 5 6 7	1 2 3 4 5	1 2	1 2 3 4 5 6 7	1 2 3 4
4 5 6 7 8 9 10	8 9 10 11 12 13 14	6 7 8 9 10 11 12	3 4 5 6 7 8 9	8 9 10 11 12 13 14	5 6 7 8 9 10 11
11 12 13 14 15 16 17	15 16 17 18 19 20 21	13 14 15 16 17 18 19	10 11 12 13 14 15 16	15 16 17 18 19 20 21	12 13 14 15 16 17 18
18 19 20 21 22 23 24	22 23 24 25 26 27 28	20 21 22 23 24 25 26	17 18 19 20 21 22 23	22 23 24 25 26 27 28	19 20 21 22 23 24 25
25 26 27 28 29 30 31	29 30	27 28 29 30 31	24 25 26 27 28 29 30	29 30 31	26 27 28 29 30 31

February	March	April	May	June	July
S M T W T F S	S M T W T F S	S M T W T F S	S M T W T F S	S M T W T F S	S M T W T F S
1	1	1 2 3 4 5	1 2 3	1 2 3 4 5 6 7	1 2 3 4 5
2 3 4 5 6 7 8	2 3 4 5 6 7 8	6 7 8 9 10 11 12	4 5 6 7 8 9 10	8 9 10 11 12 13 14	6 7 8 9 10 11 12
9 10 11 12 13 14 15	9 10 11 12 13 14 15	13 14 15 16 17 18 19	11 12 13 14 15 16 17	15 16 17 18 19 20 21	13 14 15 16 17 18 19
16 17 18 19 20 21 22	16 17 18 19 20 21 22	20 21 22 23 24 25 26	18 19 20 21 22 23 24	22 23 24 25 26 27 28	20 21 22 23 24 25 26
23 24 25 26 27 28	23 24 25 26 27 28 29 30 31	27 28 29 30	25 26 27 28 29 30 31	29 30	27 28 29 30 31

Notes: _____

2025 ✦ 2026

August	September	October	November	December	January
S M T W T F S	S M T W T F S	S M T W T F S	S M T W T F S	S M T W T F S	S M T W T F S
1 2	1 2 3 4 5 6	1 2 3 4	1	1 2 3 4 5 6	1 2 3
3 4 5 6 7 8 9	7 8 9 10 11 12 13	5 6 7 8 9 10 11	2 3 4 5 6 7 8	7 8 9 10 11 12 13	4 5 6 7 8 9 10
10 11 12 13 14 15 16	14 15 16 17 18 19 20	12 13 14 15 16 17 18	9 10 11 12 13 14 15	14 15 16 17 18 19 20	11 12 13 14 15 16 17
17 18 19 20 21 22 23	21 22 23 24 25 26 27	19 20 21 22 23 24 25	16 17 18 19 20 21 22	21 22 23 24 25 26 27	18 19 20 21 22 23 24
24 25 26 27 28 29 30	28 29 30	26 27 28 29 30 31	23 24 25 26 27 28 29 30	28 29 30 31	25 26 27 28 29 30 31
31					

February	March	April	May	June	July
S M T W T F S	S M T W T F S	S M T W T F S	S M T W T F S	S M T W T F S	S M T W T F S
1 2 3 4 5 6 7	1 2 3 4 5 6 7	1 2 3 4	1 2	1 2 3 4 5 6	1 2 3 4
8 9 10 11 12 13 14	8 9 10 11 12 13 14	5 6 7 8 9 10 11	3 4 5 6 7 8 9	7 8 9 10 11 12 13	5 6 7 8 9 10 11
15 16 17 18 19 20 21	15 16 17 18 19 20 21	12 13 14 15 16 17 18	10 11 12 13 14 15 16	14 15 16 17 18 19 20	12 13 14 15 16 17 18
22 23 24 25 26 27 28	22 23 24 25 26 27 28	19 20 21 22 23 24 25	17 18 19 20 21 22 23	21 22 23 24 25 26 27	19 20 21 22 23 24 25
	29 30 31	26 27 28 29 30	24 25 26 27 28 29 30 31	28 29 30	26 27 28 29 30 31

Notes: _____

2026 ✦ 2027

August	September	October	November	December	January
S M T W T F S	S M T W T F S	S M T W T F S	S M T W T F S	S M T W T F S	S M T W T F S
1	1 2 3 4 5	1 2 3	1 2 3 4 5 6 7	1 2 3 4 5	1 2
2 3 4 5 6 7 8	6 7 8 9 10 11 12	4 5 6 7 8 9 10	8 9 10 11 12 13 14	6 7 8 9 10 11 12	3 4 5 6 7 8 9
9 10 11 12 13 14 15	13 14 15 16 17 18 19	11 12 13 14 15 16 17	15 16 17 18 19 20 21	13 14 15 16 17 18 19	10 11 12 13 14 15 16
16 17 18 19 20 21 22	20 21 22 23 24 25 26	18 19 20 21 22 23 24	22 23 24 25 26 27 28	20 21 22 23 24 25 26	17 18 19 20 21 22 23
23 24 25 26 27 28 29	27 28 29 30	25 26 27 28 29 30 31	29 30	27 28 29 30 31	24 25 26 27 28 29 30
30 31					31

February	March	April	May	June	July
S M T W T F S	S M T W T F S	S M T W T F S	S M T W T F S	S M T W T F S	S M T W T F S
1 2 3 4 5 6	1 2 3 4 5 6	1 2 3	1	1 2 3 4 5	1 2 3
7 8 9 10 11 12 13	7 8 9 10 11 12 13	4 5 6 7 8 9 10	2 3 4 5 6 7 8	6 7 8 9 10 11 12	4 5 6 7 8 9 10
14 15 16 17 18 19 20	14 15 16 17 18 19 20	11 12 13 14 15 16 17	9 10 11 12 13 14 15	13 14 15 16 17 18 19	11 12 13 14 15 16 17
21 22 23 24 25 26 27	21 22 23 24 25 26 27	18 19 20 21 22 23 24	16 17 18 19 20 21 22	20 21 22 23 24 25 26	18 19 20 21 22 23 24
28	28 29 30 31	25 26 27 28 29 30	23 24 25 26 27 28 29 30 31	27 28 29 30	25 26 27 28 29 30 31

Notes: _____

Monthly Calendars

Sun	Mon	Tue	Wed	Thu	Fri	Sat

Sun	Mon	Tue	Wed	Thu	Fri	Sat

	Sun	Mon	Tue	Wed	Thu	Fri	Sat

	Sun	Mon	Tue	Wed	Thu	Fri	Sat

Sun	**Mon**	**Tue**	**Wed**	**Thu**	**Fri**	**Sat**

Sun	**Mon**	**Tue**	**Wed**	**Thu**	**Fri**	**Sat**

Sun	**Mon**	**Tue**	**Wed**	**Thu**	**Fri**	**Sat**

Sun	**Mon**	**Tue**	**Wed**	**Thu**	**Fri**	**Sat**

Sun	**Mon**	**Tue**	**Wed**	**Thu**	**Fri**	**Sat**

Sun	**Mon**	**Tue**	**Wed**	**Thu**	**Fri**	**Sat**

Sun	Mon	Tue	Wed	Thu	Fri	Sat

Sun	Mon	Tue	Wed	Thu	Fri	Sat

Weekly Plan   Dates:_____

	22

Weekly Plan   Dates:_____

Notes

Weekly Plan   Dates:_____

Notes

Weekly Plan   Dates:_____

Weekly Plan   Dates:_____

Notes

Weekly Plan   Dates:_____

	32

Notes

Weekly Plan   Dates: _____

Notes

Weekly Plan   Dates:_____

		35	

Notes

Weekly Plan   Dates:_____

Notes

Weekly Plan   Dates:_____

Weekly Plan   Dates:_____

Notes

Weekly Plan   Dates:_____

Weekly Plan   Dates:_____

Notes

Weekly Plan   Dates:_____

Notes

Weekly Plan   Dates:_____

Notes

Weekly Plan   Dates:_____

Weekly Plan Dates:_____

Weekly Plan   Dates: _____

Notes

Weekly Plan   Dates:_____

Notes

Weekly Plan   Dates:_____

Notes

Weekly Plan   Dates:_____

Notes

Weekly Plan   Dates: _____

Notes

Weekly Plan   Dates:_____

Notes

Weekly Plan   Dates:_____

Notes

Weekly Plan   Dates:_____

Weekly Plan   Dates:_____

	72	**Notes**

Weekly Plan   Dates:_____

Notes

Weekly Plan   Dates:_____

Notes

Weekly Plan   Dates:_____

Notes

Weekly Plan   Dates:_____

Weekly Plan   Dates:_____

Weekly Plan   **Dates:** _____

Notes

Weekly Plan   Dates:_____

Notes

Weekly Plan   Dates:_____

Weekly Plan   Dates:_____

Notes

Weekly Plan   Dates:_____

Weekly Plan   Dates:_____

Notes

Weekly Plan   Dates: _____

Notes

Weekly Plan   Dates:_____

	98

Notes

Weekly Plan   Dates:_____

Notes

Weekly Plan   Dates:_____

Notes

Weekly Plan   Dates: _____

Notes

Weekly Plan   Dates:_____

Notes

Weekly Plan   Dates:_____

Notes

Weekly Plan   Dates:_____

	110

Notes

Weekly Plan   Dates:_____

Notes

Weekly Plan   Dates:_____

Weekly Plan   Dates:_____

Notes

Weekly Plan   Dates:_____

Notes

Weekly Plan   Dates: _____

Notes

Weekly Plan   Dates:_____

Weekly Plan   Dates:_____

Notes

Future Goals

Student	Subject	Goal
Student	Subject	

Helpful Hints

Plan. Set quarterly and yearly goals for each child. Be realistic with your expectations. Refer to the goals on a regular basis and evaluate how things are going. Readjust and rewrite goals as needed.

Research. Make sure you understand your state's homeschool laws. Before committing to a curriculum or homeschool method, research your options. Mix and match materials to suit your needs. Remember that preowned books can work just as well as new.

Organize. Assign a designated space in your home to store books and school supplies. Encourage your children to return items to the designated spot so the supplies will always be easy to find.

Forget the school model. Don't try to replicate a traditional classroom setting. School can take place sitting at a kitchen table or on a living room sofa. Or school can be outside on a porch. Do what works for your family.

Create a routine. Stick to a basic daily schedule. Begin school at about the same time each day and stop at about the same time. If the work is done early, you can end your school day early. This helps motivate kids to stay on task during school.

Keep it fun. Children can be more cooperative when they enjoy an activity. Look for ways to keep kids engaged. You'll likely have more fun too.

Stay flexible. Don't be afraid to stop what you're working on and begin something else. There will be days when homeschooling is hard. You can always go back to a challenging lesson on another day.

Take breaks. Sometimes you will need a break, and sometimes your kids will need a break. Spending a few minutes outside can help. If you notice that your child is fidgety, stop the schoolwork and spend some time outdoors.

Join others. Look for opportunities to spend time with others. It helps break up the week. You can join homeschool groups, teams, or other community groups. Or visit with friends or extended family.

Don't get attached. If a curriculum or teaching method isn't working, choose something else. You may feel uneasy quitting a program that you've paid for, but it's not worth forcing something that isn't right. Maybe it will be right in the future. Maybe it won't. Every family is unique. Use what works and move on from things that don't.

Get help. If you feel overwhelmed at the thought of teaching a particular subject, get help. Use online courses for subjects that you don't want to teach, find a group class, or ask someone else to teach these subjects.

Enjoy special days. Adjust your schedule during holiday seasons and other special days to allow for more enjoyment and less stress. Put the regular work aside and do special fun activities together during these times.

Avoid comparison. It's great to speak with other homeschool parents, but don't let what they're doing interfere with what you're doing. You are not in a competition. Stick with your plans and don't worry about anyone else.

Measure progress, your way. Each state has its own guidelines, but some allow for multiple assessment methods. There are many ways to measure learning. Don't limit yourself, and your children, by only using tests.

Prioritize what matters. Each homeschool will put more emphasis on some areas and less on others. There is no one right way to homeschool. Determine what matters to your family and adjust your plan accordingly.

Fun Diversions

Guessing games. Think of a number, color, fruit, or anything else, and ask kids to guess what you're thinking. You can adjust the difficulty level as needed. Take turns with the roles of thinker and guesser.

Nature walks. Go outside and observe nature. Listen for noises and try to identify them. Or look for interesting colors, patterns, and textures.

Jokes. Take turns telling jokes.

Board games. Play a board game. Or create one together.

Cards. Play a card game that involves strategy, number comparison, or matching.

Movement. Memorization and movement work well together. Instead of sitting while reciting something, have kids hop each time they answer. Or do some jumping jacks.

Storytelling. Begin a story verbally and take turns adding to it.

Reading. Read a book together.

Music. Listen to music. Sing. Play instruments. Tap or stomp feet.

Charades. Take turns acting out something for others to guess.

Puzzle. Do a jigsaw puzzle, brain teaser, crossword, or other puzzles.

Video. Watch a short video. Or make one together.

Art. Draw, paint, sculpt, or craft something.

Dance. Listen to some upbeat music and dance.

Food. Bake, cook, or assemble a tasty treat together.

Class Ideas for Groups

- Architecture
- Acoustics
- Animals
- Art History
- Art Methods
- Baking
- Basic Chemistry
- Basic Sewing
- Bubbles
- Calligraphy
- Chocolate/Cake Decorating
- Cinematography
- Cooking
- Creative Communication
- Creative Writing
- Crochet
- Cultural Fair
- Debate
- Dissection
- Dough Class
- Drama Methods
- Duct Tape Crafts
- Elections
- Engineering
- Financial Literacy
- First Aid
- Geography through Art
- Global Art
- Graphic Arts
- Green Thumb
- Insects and Flowers
- Irish Step Dance
- International Cooking
- Kitchen Chemistry
- Knitting
- Lab Reports
- Lego Free Challenge
- Lego Simple Machines
- Map Skills
- Math Activities
- Mock Trial
- Multimedia Presentations
- Music History & Appreciation
- Music Theory & Voice
- Novel Writing
- Painting
- Paper Airplanes
- Physical Education
- Play Dough Economics
- Playground Games
- Poetry Memorization
- Preschool Music & Movement
- Presentations/Public Speaking
- Recycling Crafts
- Research Paper Writing
- Rocket Science
- Science Experiments
- Science Fair
- Sign Language
- Simple Carpentry
- Spelling Bee
- Sports History
- Story Time
- Strategy Games
- Team Building/Construction
- Weather and Seasons
- Westward Expansion
- Woodcarving

Homeschooling Resources

Visit heidikinney.com/homeschoolplanner for clickable links to these resources.

Legal Information and Assistance

Home School Legal Defense Association
(hslda.org)

The Coalition for Responsible Home Education
(responsiblehomeschooling.org)

Popular Teaching Styles

Charlotte Mason
(simplycharlottemason.com)

Leadership Education
(tjed.org)

Classical
(welltrainedmind.com)

Montessori
(livingmontessorinow.com)

Interest-Led Learning
(johnholtgws.com)

Waldorf
(whywaldorfworks.org)

Free Online Lessons and Curriculum

826 Digital
(826digital.com)

Khan Academy
(khanacademy.org)

Academic Earth
(academicearth.org)

NASA for Students
(nasa.gov/audience/forstudents/index.html)

Ambleside Online
(amblesideonline.org)

National Geographic Kids
(kids.nationalgeographic.com)

CK-12
(www.ck12.org)

PBS Learning Media
(pbslearningmedia.org)

Code.org
(code.org)

Project Gutenberg
(gutenberg.org)

Coursera/edX
(edx.org)

Smithsonian Learning Lab
(learninglab.si.edu)

Discovery Education
(discoveryeducation.com)

Storyline
(storylineonline.net)

Discovery K12
(discoveryk12.com/dk12/)

TED-Ed
(ed.ted.com)

Easy Peasy All-in-One Homeschool
(allinonehomeschool.com)

U.S. Forest Service
(fs.usda.gov/learn/educators)

Exploratorium
(exploratorium.edu/explore/activities)

XtraMath
(xtramath.org)

Funbrain
(funbrain.com)

Author's Note

Thank you for choosing this planner!

If you like the *All I Need to Homeschool Planner*, please help others find it by leaving a review online where you purchased it. Thank you!

You can learn more about me and my writing, and subscribe to my monthly newsletter, by visiting heidikinney.com.

~ Heidi

Follow me at:

facebook.com/HKinneyWriter

instagram.com/hkinneywriter